SNAKE

Selina Wood

W

FRANKLIN WATTS

LONDON•SYDNEY

First published in 2007 by Franklin Watts
338 Euston Road, London NW1 3BH

Franklin Watts Australia
Level 17/207 Kent Street
Sydney NSW 2000

Editor: Rachel Tonkin and Julia Bird
Designer: Proof Books
Picture researcher: Diana Morris

Picture credits:
José Bergada/PD: 25, 29; Georgette Douwma/ Nature PL: 6;
Laura Dwight/Corbis: 11; Jenny Fowler/PD: front cover.
Daniel Heuclin/NHPA: 10; Michael Hutchinson/Nature PL: 4.
Neal & Molly Jansen/Alamy: 18; Juniors Bildarchiv/Alamy: 19.
Chris Mattison/PD: 5, 13; Barll Pascal/KIPA/Corbis: 27.
Hugh Penney/PD: 20; E. Hanumantha Rao/NHPA: 9; Kim Taylor/
Nature PL: 21; Robert Valentic/ Nature PL: 8; Barrie Watts/Alamy: 24;
Martin Wendler/NHPA: 7; Paul Wood/Alamy: 12.

All other photography: Andy Crawford
With thanks to Mitch and Hazel Price at The Reptile Experience

Every attempt has been made to clear copyright.
Should there be any inadvertent omission please
apply to the publisher for rectification.

A CIP catalogue record for this book
is available from the British Library

ISBN: 978 0 7496 7058 0

Dewey Classification: 636.3'96

Printed in China

Franklin Watts is a division of Hachette Children's Books,
an Hachette Livre UK company.

Contents

The world of snakes

Snakes are unusual and mysterious. Silent and slithering, they are captivating to watch. With the care and attention of a good owner, snakes can make interesting and rewarding pets.

Reptiles

Snakes belong to the reptile family. Reptiles are animals with bony skeletons and backbones, and skin made of scales. They are cold-blooded, which means their body temperature becomes the same as the temperature of their surroundings. Snakes have no legs or eyelids. They range in size from the thread snake, which can be only 11cm long, to the reticulated python, which can grow up to 10m.

Slender, burrowing thread snakes are some of the smallest snakes in the world.

Moving along

Attached to a snake's backbone are muscles that allow the snake to twist into coils and wriggle along. Some snakes move forward by waving their body from side to side, while others slither along in a concertina-like action.

Snake senses

Snakes' eyesight is not very good and they do not have external ears. Instead, they hear by picking up vibrations with their skin and muscles, which are then passed on to an inner ear. Their skin is also very sensitive to touch and slight changes in temperature. Snakes have nostrils, but they smell by picking up particles in the air with their long, forked tongue. They press the particles against a special organ on the roof of the mouth, called the Jacobson's Organ, which detects the 'smell' of the particles.

Expert predators

All snakes are carnivorous, meaning that their diet consists of other animals. Many snakes immobilise their prey before eating it, either with a type of poison, called venom, or by suffocation. There are about 600 species of venomous snake, including snakes from the cobra and viper families. They inject poison into their prey through grooved or hollow teeth called fangs. Venom is a type of saliva produced in a gland on the roof of a snake's mouth.

A rattlesnake (a type of viper) shows off its fangs.

Silent snakes

Snakes are silent most of the time but some will hiss if they feel threatened. Other snakes, such as rattlesnakes, rattle their tails to warn predators to stay away.

Amazing jaws

Snakes do not eat often, around once a week to once a month depending on the species, but they can consume large amounts in one meal. Snakes' jaws are elastic and can stretch very wide, allowing them to swallow whole animals, often bigger than their head.

Questions & Answers

✴ **What do snakes eat?**
In the wild, small snakes feed on insects, snails and flies while medium-sized snakes eat birds, mice and frogs. Large snakes can devour large mammals, sometimes as big as antelopes, as well as other snakes.

✴ **How do snakes reproduce?**
Most snakes lay eggs but some types, such as boas, give birth to live young.

✴ **How does venom kill?**
It can either paralyse muscles and stop the heart and lungs from working or damage blood vessels and body tissue.

Snakes in the wild

There are over 2,700 known snake species in the world, and they live on all continents except Antarctica. Most live in hot, tropical regions. Snakes thrive in a variety of habitats – in trees, underground burrows, vegetation and even in the sea.

Sea kraits live in tropical oceans where they feed on fish. They return to the shore to lay their eggs.

Escaping predators

Snakes use various methods to escape from predators. Most have camouflaged skin so they can merge into their surroundings. Coral snakes, on the other hand, are brightly coloured to warn predators they are venomous. Snakes can also make themselves look big, hiss or even let off a foul smell. Some, such as the grass snake, pretend to be dead. Only in the last resort do most snakes bite.

Habitats

All snakes are a similar shape, but their bodies have adapted to where they live. Burrowing snakes have rounded bodies to tunnel through soil, while tree snakes have long tails to help them climb. Ground snakes have large belly scales to grip rocks and soil, and the tails of sea snakes are shaped like paddles for swimming.

Hot and cold

Snakes are cold-blooded, which means they cannot control their own body temperature. Instead, they bask in the warmth of the sun to warm them up and rely on the shade to cool them down. Snakes that live in colder climates brumate (hibernate) during the winter months. Some snakes that live in warmer climates are nocturnal. They are most active at night when the temperature is lower.

Death by constriction

The world's biggest snakes are the boas of South America and the pythons of Africa and Asia. Boas kill their prey by constriction, or suffocation. After seizing prey with its sharp teeth, a constrictor wraps its body around its victim several times. Every time the animal breathes out, the snake squeezes more and more tightly, until its prey eventually dies of suffocation.

The anaconda is an enormous type of boa. It lives in the rivers and swamps of South America, and feeds on large prey such as caiman (alligators).

Questions & Answers

✳ **Which animals hunt snakes?**
Snakes are preyed upon by birds of prey, crocodiles, mammals such as foxes, raccoons and mongooses, and of course, humans.

✳ **Which are the most venomous snakes?**
The African Black mamba, Indian Cobra and Australian Tiger snake are all highly dangerous.

✳ **Is there anywhere with no snakes?**
Yes, apart from Antarctica, some islands such as Ireland and New Zealand do not have snakes in the wild.

Black magic

The fastest land snake is the African Black Mamba. It can move at a speed of 11km per hour.

Heat seekers

Some snakes are able to detect the location of their prey by the body heat it gives out. Pit vipers, for example, have two heat-sensitive organs located on either side of their head. Even in the dark, these snakes can tell if warm-blooded prey is nearby.

Snakes as pets

If you are thinking of buying a snake to keep as a pet, find out as much as you can about them before you obtain one. Remember that looking after a snake is a long-term commitment.

Choose carefully

First of all, choose your snake carefully. Some snakes, particularly the poisonous ones, are very dangerous and should be left to the experts. Pythons, although not poisonous, can be moody, so are not ideal pets if you have never owned a snake before. Large snakes, such as the boa constrictor, can grow to be several metres long and may be a little tricky to house and handle! Some good 'starter' snakes are suggested on pages 10-11.

What a snake needs

Remember you will need to provide your pet snake with food, shelter and health care throughout its life. Find out how long your snake will be likely to live (snakes live anywhere from 10 to 25 years on average), how much it will cost to keep and think about who can look after your snake when you go on holiday. Remember that snakes and other pets, such as dogs, don't always mix.

The right pet for you?

Snakes can be beautiful and are fascinating to watch. They are very quiet pets and do not need to be taken for walks. They are quite easy to keep clean, too. But you can't cuddle a snake, and when they are frightened they can be aggressive. They need specialist equipment and their diet, which includes dead mice, can put people off.

The bite of the Australian Tiger snake can be fatal to humans. These snakes should never be kept as pets.

Endangered snakes

Snakes have always been killed because humans are afraid of them. Snakes are also hunted for their skins and for the pet trade, while their habitats in the wild are under increasing threat. Recently, laws have been introduced to protect endangered snakes, so you should check whether you need a permit from your local government authority or a national animal welfare organisation before buying your pet. Several types of snake, including the Indian Python, are protected under The Convention on International Trade in Endangered Species (CITES). Now only Indian pythons that have been bred in captivity can be bought and sold.

Pet research

Find out all you can about pet snakes from the Internet, books and magazines, local or national reptile societies and from animal welfare organisations. Ask people you know who already keep snakes for their advice.

Wild side

Snakes born in captivity make the best pets. Snakes taken from the wild can be nervous, prone to diseases, and difficult to feed.

An Indian python drapes itself along a branch in its natural tree habitat. Indian pythons are now protected in the wild.

Starter snakes

There are many types of snake available to buy, but if you have never owned one before it is best to begin with a small, gentle snake that is relatively easy to look after.

Corn snakes are keen climbers in their natural habitat – the woodlands and fields of the eastern United States.

Corn snakes

Corn snakes make good starter snakes. They are colourful, medium-sized snakes that grow to about one metre long. They are non-venomous, docile and easy to feed. They are also not too expensive to buy. In the wild they mostly live on the ground, but are good climbers, too. They are very agile snakes and can easily get through small gaps, so make sure you keep them in a secure environment. Corn snakes are nocturnal – they are most active at night, in the early morning or in the late evening.

Different varieties

In the wild, corn snakes have a pinkish-orange body marked with brown blotches. In captivity they have been bred to be lots of different colours. You can get corn snakes that are completely white (albino) or black, or others that have striking black and white patterns. Young corn snakes are grey-brown; they do not have colour markings until they are adults.

Rat snakes and king snakes

Other snakes that make good pets are rat snakes and king snakes. Both these species are found across the United States. Rat snakes are related to the corn snake, but can grow up to two metres long and are more active during the day. They live in wooded regions in the wild. King snakes grow to just over a metre long. They enjoy being handled once tamed, like small enclosures and are not fussy eaters. They come in a range of colours and markings.

Remember!

Whatever type of snake you get, make sure you know about its specific needs before you buy it. Snakes are very sensitive to changes in their environment, such as heat and light, and can suffer if the conditions they live in aren't just right.

Once tamed, a king snake will be friendly and curious.

Questions & Answers

✳ **How long do corn snakes live?**
Corn snakes can live for 10–15 years.

✳ **Where should I keep my corn snake?**
Corn snakes are nocturnal, so you should put them in a quiet place where they are not disturbed too much during the day.

✳ **Should I buy a male or a female snake?**
There is little difference in temperament between males and females. In appearance, the tail of most male snakes is slightly thicker and longer than the female of the species.

Choosing your snake

Once you have found out all you can about keeping a snake, your next step is to find a good specialist pet shop or reptile breeder where you can find the snake that you want and buy the right equipment.

A snake from a good breeder or pet shop should be used to being handled.

Where can I buy a snake?

You can find out about reptile breeders and specialist pet shops on the Internet, through reptile magazines and through your local or national herpetological or reptile and amphibian society (see page 31). You can also get in touch with your local vet or an animal welfare organisation for advice on breeders. A good pet shop or breeder will look after their animals well, and should care about their animals' futures. You could also visit an animal rescue shelter. However, a snake from an animal shelter may be less easy to tame than one bought from a breeder.

Ask questions

When you go to a pet shop or reptile breeder, check whether the animals are being properly cared for. The tanks should look clean and the animals healthy. Ask the breeder lots of questions. Find out about the snake's history, how old the snake is, what it likes to eat and how often it should be fed. You will also want to know how often your snake is losing its skin or shedding (see page 25). A healthy snake should not have problems shedding. It is also important to check that the snakes have been bred in captivity.

Things to watch out for…

Avoid a snake that:

* is inactive and sleepy
* has mites on its body
* has bumps or cuts on its body or bits of shed skin stuck to it
* has pinkish scales on its belly, which may indicate an infection
* does not flick its tongue when it moves around
* seems nervous or agitated.

A healthy snake should have shiny scales and bright eyes, like this young king snake.

Questions & Answers

* **How should I take my snake home?**

  For short journeys you can put your new pet in a secure cloth bag. For longer journeys, you should use a ventilated plastic box (available from specialist pet shops) and make sure it is heated to the correct temperature (see page 17).

* **Should I buy a young or an older snake?**

  It is best to buy a young snake (ideally around a year old) so that it can get used to you at an early age and is easier to tame.

* **How will I know what equipment I need?**

  A good pet shop or breeder should be able to advise you on the sort of tank and equipment your snake needs and be able to sell it to you. It is a good idea to set up the tank in the right conditions before you get your pet home (see page 16).

Snake selection

There may be a large selection of snakes at the breeder. Look for the species of snake that you have researched, and try to find an alert and active young snake with shiny scales.

Fast growers

Corn snakes can grow up to 60cm by the time they are a year old. They grow to their full size after about five years.

Handling your snake

When you get your snake you will probably be very keen to pick it up to see what it feels like and how it moves. But you should take a few moments to learn how to handle and respond to it properly first.

Easy does it

At first your snake will probably be a little frightened of you and can try to slither away and hide if you go near it. It may think that you are a dangerous predator! It is a good idea to move your hand around slowly in your snake's container or tank before you touch it. Your snake will gradually realise your hand is not going to harm it.

Let your snake get used to your presence gradually.

Taming it

When your snake is used to your hand, slowly try to touch it. Stroke it with your finger at first. Don't make jerky or sudden movements and keep quiet. If your snake seems relaxed, then try picking it up. Remember snakes don't want to be picked up all the time! They need peace and quiet, particularly when they are sleeping, have just eaten or are shedding their skin.

Snake proof!

Before you try to take your new pet out of the tank, you should make sure that there aren't any gaps or spaces in the room that your snake could disappear into. Bear in mind that snakes can squeeze into surprisingly small places! Close off any gaps and remember to remove any sharp objects that could injure your pet.

Lifting it up

The best way to hold a snake is with two hands, one behind the head, with the other hand supporting the rest of the body. Hold it close to your body, so that you and the snake feel secure, and place something soft under you in case the snake falls. Once it gets used to you, your snake may start to crawl around up your arms or even under your clothes. If it flicks out its tongue towards you when you are holding it, don't be afraid, it is just trying to smell you!

Questions & Answers

* **My snake tries to get away when I pick it up. What should I do?**
  Maybe your snake isn't comfortable enough in your hands. Put it back in its tank to relax. After a few days, try stroking it gently with your hand before picking it up again.

* **Is it hygienic to pick up my snake?**
  It is quite safe enough, but make sure you wash your hands after you have held your snake, and do not eat or drink when you are handling it, as snakes can carry harmful bacteria. Do not let your snake slither across kitchen surfaces either.

* **Will my snake bite?**
  It shouldn't bite if you are gentle with it, but occasionally it might if it is frightened or mistakes your hand for food. It is also not a good idea to pick a snake up when it is shedding. See more on snake bites on pages 24–25.

Hold your snake gently, using both hands for extra support.

Getting used to you

If you are gentle with your snake and handle it regularly, it should get used to you, and after a few weeks will feel relaxed in your hands. This will be helpful if you need to move your snake to clean the tank, or if you need to examine the snake in an emergency.

Late riser

If your snake is nocturnal, it is best to handle it in the evening to cause it the least possible disturbance.

Creating a home

When you first bring your snake home it may be anxious and nervous. Have everything set up before it arrives so that it is disturbed as little as possible and can quickly settle into its new surroundings.

Tanks

There are several different types of snake tanks, or vivaria, available, ranging from glass tanks, similar to fish tanks, to larger enclosures with sliding doors. Find out which is the best match for the age and type of your snake. Put the tank somewhere stable where it can't be knocked over, out of direct sunlight, but somewhere not too cold either. Make sure the hinges, locks and top of the snake's tank are secure so your snake can't escape.

A suitable tank set-up for a baby snake should include plenty of substrate, somewhere to shelter, a water dish and a heating pad.

Beware!

Avoid using a mesh-lined cage for snakes. These cages cannot keep the temperature constant and could injure your snake if it tried to climb through the mesh. Remember to take anything with sharp edges that could injure your snake out of the tank too.

Inside the tank

Cover the floor of the tank with material, called substrate, to keep your snake comfortable and warm. The best material for this is newspaper or paper towels, but you can also buy pre-packed wood cuts and shavings from specialist pet stores. Cut the paper or towels into pieces to fit the tank and then layer them on top of each other so that when the snake soils the paper, the top layer can easily be removed.

Keep it warm

The temperature of the tank should always be kept close to the temperature of the snake's natural habitat in the wild. This temperature will depend on the kind of snake you are keeping. Tropical snakes, for example, such as boa constrictors and pythons, need constant daytime temperatures of about 27°C. Corn snakes require an average temperature range of 25–30°C in the summer, cooling to 20°C in the winter.

Hot spots

Small tanks can be heated with a heating pad directly beneath them, while bigger enclosures may need a heat lamp or heater with a thermostat. You should set up the heating system so that some areas of the tank are warmer than others. In the wild, a snake basks in the sun to become active, then finds a shady spot to cool down when it becomes too hot. You should try to mimic these conditions in the tank.

Questions & Answers

✳ **How big should the tank be?**
The tank needs to be big enough for the snake to stretch out and turn around in and deep enough for it to move vertically, too. The tanks of baby snakes should not be too big as they like to feel secure in a small, enclosed space.

✳ **Is heating the tank important?**
Yes, it is. You should check the temperature of different parts of the tank regularly with a thermometer. A snake can die if it gets too hot or too cold. For corn snakes, no part of the tank should be lower than 20°C.

✳ **Can I use gravel or cat litter to cover the tank's floor?**
No, these materials trap moisture and filth and they can cause serious harm if they are eaten by the snake. Do not use cedar wood shavings either, as these can be poisonous to the snake.

It is very important to get the correct light and heating in your tank to keep your snake happy and healthy.

Tank accessories

To keep your snake comfortable and healthy, make the conditions of the tank as near as possible to what your snake would experience in the wild. Set the tank up step by step.

Water bowl

A water bowl is essential as all snakes require fresh water to drink. A heavy bowl is best so that your pet doesn't tip it over. Some snakes like to soak in their bowls too, as this can help them shed their skin. Make sure you change the water in the bowl every day. The replacement water should be about room temperature.

This snake is using the moisture in its water dish to help shed its skin.

Humidity

It is important to carefully maintain the right levels of ventilation and humidity in the tank. If the air is too dry, your snake may have trouble shedding its skin; too wet and the substrate may get mouldy, encouraging fungi and bacteria to build up. You can check humidity levels with an instrument called a hygrometer. If necessary, spray a little water on the substrate to increase the humidity level.

Lighting

Ideally snakes need natural sunlight every day, but this is not always practical. The best solution is to use an artificial ultraviolet light. These are available from most good pet shops. The light should be on for about 10–12 hours each day, after which snakes need darkness. Corn snakes, which are nocturnal, prefer only eight hours of sunlight during the winter.

Shelters and rocks

Snakes also need at least one covered area, or shelter, to rest and hide in. This helps to make them feel secure. Shelters can be bought from pet shops, but you can also make them out of toilet-roll tubes, small cardboard boxes or huddles of branches and rocks. Try to put one in the warm area of the tank, and another in the cool part.

Rough surfaces

Snakes also need a hard, rough object to rub against when they start shedding their skin. Rocks and branches are good for this and also make the tank look attractive. Be careful not to clutter the cage up though, as it will reduce space and mean more cleaning, and make sure there aren't any sharp edges that could injure your snake.

Climbers

Corn snakes are keen climbers in the wild. When your snake is big enough, you may want to get a deeper tank so that you can add some vertical branches that your snake can climb. Make sure you wash any branches you pick up outside before you put them in the tank so you don't bring germs into the tank.

A snake should have somewhere to shelter in its tank.

Questions & Answers

✳ **Can I put plants in my tank?**
Yes, they can make a tank look very attractive, but make sure the plants won't be poisonous to your snake and bear in mind that they are difficult to keep healthy. You could add plastic plants instead.

✳ **Can I keep more than one snake in the same tank?**
Corn snakes are solitary in the wild, but it is possible to house small groups of snakes together providing they have adequate space. You should seek expert advice first.

✳ **Can I change the arrangement of the tank sometimes?**
Yes, as long as a snake still has all the main components of a tank that it needs. A snake can benefit from having an occasional change in surroundings. Don't move things around too often though, or your snake may get unsettled.

Feeding your pet

Feeding your snake can be one of the most exciting aspects of looking after it. It can be fascinating watching how snakes eat. Make sure you feed it the correct food at the right intervals to keep it healthy.

Feeding time

Corn snakes eat insects, such as crickets and small frozen mice. Both of these are available from specialist pet shops and reptile breeders. Once you place the food in the tank, watch your snake smell, grab and gradually swallow it. It is astonishing how much they can gulp up in one go!

Watch your fingers!

Be careful when you feed your snake. Do not hold the food in your fingers when offering it to your snake. You might get your fingers bitten! Use tongs and leave it in the cage for your pet to snap up at its leisure.

Amazing eaters

Snakes eat their prey whole and can digest all parts except hair and feathers. They can digest bones within 72 hours.

Keep it real

Young corn snakes like to eat crickets and very small frozen mice called pinkies. Always defrost the mice thoroughly (ask an adult to help you) before you give them to your snake but do not cook them. Snakes are used to eating warm, live food, so you may want to mimic this by placing the defrosted food in a warm bowl of water before feeding it to your snake.

A king snake stretches its jaws wide to swallow up a mouse.

How much and when?

Snakes digest their food slowly, so you don't need to feed your snake very often (around once a week for young snakes; once every two or three weeks for older ones), but make sure you feed them the correct quantity. Be careful not to overfeed your snake or it will become ill. It is a good idea to keep a record of when you feed your snake so you don't lose track.

Suggested feeding amounts

Very young snake – one pinkie or five to ten crickets once a week

A juvenile snake (under a year old) – one large mouse every seven to ten days

An adult snake (depending on size) – two large mice or one rat once every two to three weeks

For nocturnal snakes, the best time to feed your snake is early in the day or late in the evening.

Questions & Answers

✴ **What if my snake doesn't eat the food I've given it?**
You may need to encourage it to eat. Use tongs to move the prey around to make it look as if it is live prey. You could also get help to open up the mouse so that the snake can smell it better.

✴ **What else can I feed my snake?**
For variety, you can feed your snake frozen chicks or quail eggs. You can also buy special snake sausages, which have added nutrients. Adding some variety to a snake's diet may encourage it to eat if it is going off its food. Never try to feed it bits and pieces though, as snakes need to eat the whole animal to stay healthy.

✴ **Can I feed my snake live prey?**
No, it is illegal to feed a snake live prey in the UK and many other countries.

Bulge

After your snake has swallowed its prey, you may see a bulge in its body where the prey is. The bulge will gradually get smaller as the snake's powerful digestive juices break down its meal. If the bulge is very big then your snake may be experiencing digestion problems, and you should feed it less next time.

The African egg-eating snake can swallow and digest eggs that are three times as big as its head.

21

Keeping the tank clean

One of your main responsibilities as a snake owner is to keep your pet's tank clean. It is not difficult to do and will become easier once it becomes part of your routine.

Clean up

You should give the tank a thorough clean once every two weeks. Take out all the contents of the tank, and clean them and the tank with a mild, non-toxic detergent or disinfectant. A solution of water, detergent and 5% disinfectant is usually safe, but always check first that the disinfectant won't harm your pet. Wash out the tank thoroughly with water and let it dry completely. Clean and dry the contents before putting them back in the tank. Throw away anything that cannot be cleaned easily.

Dirty tank

If you don't clean your snake's tank out regularly, a build up of fungi and bacteria in the tank can lead to your snake coming down with a disease, and can also cause germs to spread in your home. Germs can multiply if you leave uneaten food in the tank, or don't clear away your snake's faeces regularly. Poor ventilation and high levels of humidity can also cause germs to build up.

Change the substrate in your snake's tank regularly. If it looks damp or mouldy, throw it away immediately.

Temporary home

When you clean out its tank, move your snake into a separate container so that it cannot escape or get covered in disinfectant and water while you clean. A ventilated plastic box makes a good temporary home for snakes. Don't clean out the tank more than you need to however, as it will unsettle your snake. In between full tank clean-outs, get into the habit of changing the snake's water every day and regularly spot cleaning soiled substrate. You will soon get into a cleaning routine.

A ventilated plastic container with substrate makes a good temporary home for your snake.

Cleaning check list

* Change the water in your snake's water bowl every day so that it stays fresh.

* Remove faeces or soiled substrate from the tank every two days.

* Give the tank a thorough clean about once every two weeks.

* Make sure you wash your hands after cleaning to prevent you carrying germs or harmful bacteria out of the tank.

Questions & Answers

* **What should I do if there is mould or fungi in the tank?**
Clean out the tank and throw out any plants or branches that are affected. Examine your snake to make sure it looks healthy.

* **What happens if the snake gets an infestation of mites?**
Mites are pin-sized creatures, either black or red in colour, that can infest a snake or a whole tank. Seek medical advice from an expert or vet on treating the snake, and replace all the contents of the tank. You may be able to get products to prevent or treat minor outbreaks from specialist pet shops.

Snake bites

Once your snake gets to know you it should be easy to handle most of the time. Here are some suggestions as to how to avoid bites, and what to do if you do receive a nip.

A bite from a corn snake can be painful, but is not usually dangerous to humans.

Why do snakes bite?

A snake will normally only bite if it is frightened or feels threatened, or if it mistakes your hand for food. That is why it is important to let a snake get to know you gradually before attempting to pick it up. Never play around with your snake when you are holding it, as this may frighten the snake and make it bite you. Sudden jerky movements, or a fall, may also cause your snake to lash out.

What to do

Corn snakes and king snakes are not venomous and they have small teeth so they are unlikely to hurt you badly if they bite you. They might, however, be reluctant to let go! Don't be frightened and don't try to pull the snake away from you. Support the rest of your snake with your other hand and ask an adult to help you remove it. If you put your hand in a bowl of water the snake will gradually let go. Make sure you wash any bite wounds thoroughly and apply some antiseptic ointment. Then visit a doctor for a check up.

Telling tails

You may be able to tell when your snake is about to bite. Black rat snakes have scales at the end of their tail that rattle when they want to scare away predators, a bit like a rattlesnake. But unlike rattlesnakes, rat snakes are not venomous.

Fatal bite

About one in five snakes are poisonous to humans, but only a few species can actually kill.

Shedding

Snakes can be more prone to bite if you disturb them when they are shedding their skin. Snakes shed their skin as they grow, and shed more frequently when they are babies (every three to four weeks). You can tell when a snake is about to shed because its eyes go cloudy, it is inactive, and it goes off its food. It is best to leave your snake alone during this time, and for the first week or so after shedding.

Questions & Answers

✻ **How do I feed my snake without getting bitten?**
Do not give the food to your snake directly with your hands and leave the food on the floor of the tank, or in a special box for food. If you have just been handling food, wash your hands before you handle your snake. Your snake may smell the food on your hands and mistake it for more dinner!

✻ **What if my snake's teeth come off when it bites?**
It is natural for a snake's teeth to come off when they bite their prey, but they soon grow back again.

✻ **If my snake has bitten me, when should I try picking it up again?**
Don't be afraid to handle it again, but leave it for a few days and remember to be gentle with it.

This corn snake is in the process of shedding its skin. Snakes often shed their skin in one whole piece.

Signs of sickness

One of your key responsibilities as a snake owner is to look out for any signs of illness or injury. You should make a habit of doing this when you clean out the tank.

Not eating?

If your snake is not eating or drinking, examine it to see if it seems sick or is injured anywhere. Try varying your snake's diet if it won't eat and soaking it in warm water to get it to drink. (Remember that snakes may go off their food just before they shed.) If you are still experiencing problems, take it to a vet. If your snake is vomiting after eating, try feeding it less food next time, but if symptoms persist, seek advice.

Shedding problems

Snakes become less active when they are shedding their skin and that is perfectly healthy. However, if your snake has problems shedding its skin – for example, if there are bits of the old skin stuck to it, it may need some help from you. Soak your snake in water and make sure it has a rock to rub up against to help it shed. If your snake is still having problems shedding, ask for advice from a vet or a reptile society.

Sluggish and inactive

If you find your snake is sluggish and not very alert, it may be too cold. Remember your snake needs external heat in order to be active and well. Check the temperature of the tank to make sure it is correct.

Stick-on aquarium thermometers are a good way of monitoring the temperature in your tank.

Signs of illness

A healthy snake should be active, have a rounded, firm, muscular body, and taste the air regularly with its tongue. If you spot any of the signs of sickness in the list below in your pet, you should seek advice from a snake expert or vet. For the less serious illnesses, you may be able to buy treatments from a specialist reptile shop.

* Wrinkled, saggy skin

* Lumps or bumps

* Skinniness

* Change of colour

* Ticks or mites stuck to skin

* Diarrhoea

* Swollen mouth

* Wounds, such as burns, cuts or blisters

* Wheezing

Top tips

* Keep the tank clean at all times.

* Check the tank's temperature and humidity regularly.

* Feed your snake its correct diet.

* Check your snake regularly to make sure it is looking well.

* Find out as much as you can about snake diseases so you can spot tell-tale signs.

* If in any doubt, take your snake to the vet.

Zzzzz...

Snakes can become slow and inactive after eating. This is because they are using up all their energy digesting their meal!

Visiting a vet

It is a good idea to seek out a vet that has knowledge of reptile treatment as soon as you get your snake so you know where to take it in case of an emergency. Take your snake to a vet for an initial check up so that your vet can tell you that your new snake is healthy, and advise you on how to look after it. He or she will give it a thorough examination to make sure it is in good condition.

Find a vet who is experienced in handling and treating snakes.

A snake's life

If you look after your snake well, it may live for ten or more years. During this time you will develop a strong bond with your snake and will have lots of stories to tell about the time you spent with your pet.

Life span

Snakes grow throughout their lives. However, the rate at which they grow slows down a lot after the first five years or so and they shed less and less frequently. Snakes can live for longer than you might think. Corn snakes live for ten to fifteen years and some larger snakes, such as pythons and boas, can live for 25 years or more.

Keep a record

Why not keep a record of your snake's life with photos and pictures? You could also include tips on how to care for your snake, as well as information on different species of snakes in the wild. It will be an important record of your snake's well-being and interesting for you to look back on over the years.

As your snake get older its eyesight will deteriorate and its eyes may become cloudy and dull.

An old snake

Over time you will notice that your snake's behaviour may change. As your snake gets older, it may be less active and its eyes and skin may become a little dull looking. Be sensitive to its old age, do not pick it up and disturb it too much. When your snake finally dies you will feel sad, but at least you will have made the most of your time together.

Photographs of you and your pet at different stages of its life will bring back happy memories.

Questions & Answers

✳ **What is the oldest snake on record?**
The oldest snake reliably recorded is a boa constrictor named Popeye who died in Philadelphia Zoo, USA, in 1977 at the grand age of 40.

✳ **When should a snake be put to sleep?**
If your pet is very ill or old, it may be time to think about putting an end to its suffering. Your vet should be able to give you advice on the kindest thing to do.

✳ **Where can I find out more about snakes, including snakes in the wild?**
Visit your local library or bookshop to find books on snakes, and try looking on the Internet (some websites are suggested on page 31). You can also contact reptile organisations or visit the reptile houses of zoos and nature centres.

Accidents and illness

If you are unlucky and your snake dies in an accident or from illness, or you have to have your snake put down, try not to blame yourself. The chances are there was nothing you or anyone else could have done to prevent it. Talk to people about how you feel – it usually helps. You will soon be able to think about your pet with fond, happy memories.

Remembering your snake

You may want to hold a memorial service in the garden when your snake dies (but check first that you are allowed to bury pets in your area). This is a good way of showing your respect to your pet. You could also write a poem all about your snake and the memories you have of it.

Glossary

adaptations
Special features of an animal that help it thrive in its particular habitat.

albino
Animal or person with very light or white skin or hair.

bacteria
Microscopic living things, many of which can cause disease.

camouflage
Colour or markings that help something blend in with its surroundings.

captivity
Being under the control of humans.

carnivorous
Eating mainly or only meat.

cold-blooded
Having a body whose temperature varies with the environment.

constriction
Killing by suffocation.

endangered
In danger of extinction.

fungi
Spore-producing living things that feed on other living things.

gland
An organ that controls substances in the body.

habitat
A place where an animal or plant lives.

hibernate
To hide away or sleep during the cold part of the year.

humidity
The level of moisture in the air.

hygrometer
An instrument used to measure humidity.

mammal
A warm-blooded animal that produces live young, has hair and feeds its young.

mite
A tiny creature that can infest animals, plants or some foods. Many kinds of mites are also parasites (see below).

nocturnal
Active at night.

nutrients
The different components of food that give an animal energy and help to keep it well.

parasites
A living thing that feeds off and causes harm to another living thing.

reptile
A cold-blooded animal with scaly skin. Reptiles include snakes, lizards, crocodiles, turtles and tortoises.

shed
To get rid of old skin to make way for a new layer. Reptiles shed so that they can grow.

species
A group of animals that have characteristics in common, distinct from other animals, and that can reproduce together.

substrate
A layer of material at the bottom of a tank.

thermostat
A device that keeps temperature steady.

tropical
From the hot, humid climate of the tropics.

venomous
Capable of injecting venom (poison).

vivarium
A tank.

Further information

If you want to learn more about types of snakes, buying snakes, looking after snakes, or if you would like to get involved in animal welfare, these are some helpful websites:

UNITED KINGDOM
British Herpetological Society
Articles and information on the study of reptiles. Runs the Young Herpetological Society, which has educational resources and information for young fans of reptiles.
Website: www.thebhs.org
Email: info@thebhs.org
Contact address:
The British Herpetological Society
11, Strathmore Place, Montrose, Angus, United Kingdom DD10 8LQ

Reptile All Sorts
Lots of diverse information on snakes including a list of breeders, care sheets and equipment suppliers.
Website: www.reptileallsorts.com
Contact: 0191 266 6290

The Reptile Experience
A family-run company that offers tips and advice on caring for reptiles, as well as a rescue service.
Website: www.reptilehouse.net

Royal Society for the Prevention of Cruelty to Animals
News articles, rehoming information and animal care advice from the Royal Society of Cruelty to Animals
Website: www.rspca.org.uk
Contact address:
Enquiries service, RSPCA, Wilberforce Way, Southwater, Horsham, West Sussex RH13 9RS
0870 33 35 999

AUSTRALIA
Australian Herpetological Society
Society devoted to reptiles.
Website: www.ahs.org.au
Email: webmaster@ahs.org.au

Aussie Reptile Keeper
Good Australian website with useful information about keeping reptiles.
Website: www.aussiereptilekeeper.com

UNITED STATES OF AMERICA
The American Society for the Prevention of Cruelty to Animals website features pet care advice and campaigns fighting against animal cruelty.
Website: www.aspca.org

INTERNATIONAL
International Herpetological Society
Subscribe and receive regular newsletters and a reptile journal.
Website: www.international-herpetological-society.org

Website of People for the Ethical Treatment of Animals – the world's largest animal rights group. Contains information promoting the safety and responsible treatment of animals.
Website: www.peta.org

Note to parents and teachers: Every effort has been made by the Publishers to ensure that these websites are suitable for children, that they are of the highest educational value, and that they contain no inappropriate or offensive material. However, because of the nature of the Internet, it is impossible to guarantee that the contents of these sites will not be altered. We strongly advise that Internet access is supervised by a responsible adult.

Index